Samsung Galaxy S4

User Manual:

The Complete Samsung Galaxy S4
Guide To Conquer Your Device

This User Guide covers everything you need to know for you
new Samsung Galaxy S4. It encompasses basic usage to advanced
new features, and everything in between.

By Daniel Forrester

Table of Contents

Introduction

The Samsung Galaxy S4 is one of the hottest phones on the market, with an impressive screen size and resolution, amazing battery life and one of the fastest processors out there. There are so many available features that it may be tough to get the most out of your phone without some help, so this guide will help teach you the ins and outs of the Galaxy S4!

Chapter 1: Galaxy S4 vs. Galaxy S3

The Samsung Galaxy S4 is the fourth-generation version of the popular Samsung Galaxy S series of smart phones. It was released in April 2013, which was almost one full year after the Galaxy S3.

Upon its release, the Samsung Galaxy S4 was quickly regarded as one of the best smart phones on the market. It includes intuitive new features to streamline navigation, such as Smart Stay, Smart Scroll and Air Gesture. It has a 13-megapixel camera on the back and a display that measures five inches.

Screen

The screen size and resolution are two of the biggest differences between the Galaxy S4 and Galaxy S3 for most users. Samsung made some noticeable changes, increasing the screen size by two-tenths of an inch to just a touch under five inches. They were able to do this while reducing the overall size of the phone, thanks to a trimmed down bezel.

There is one drawback to the bigger screen, which is that it can be slightly more difficult to reach across the phone with your thumb or fingers to press different buttons. It takes a little bit of getting used to, but most users are happy to sacrifice the feel in order to get the extra screen size. Do expect a few extra accidental button presses in your first few weeks with the phone, though.

The resolution is upgraded to 1080p, which is 1920 pixels by 1080 pixels. That's full HD, which is up from 1280 pixels by 720 pixels.

Camera

The Galaxy S4 is one of the top camera phones on the market, with a 13-megapixel back camera. The Galaxy S3 had an 8-megapixel back camera. The front camera sees a slight upgrade, from 1.9-megapixels to 2-megapixels.

One of the cool things about the Galaxy S4's back-facing camera is that it has some software features that can enhance the quality of the photo. It offers Drama Shot, which is a burst of photos that can be combined into a single shot. Sound and Shot allows the users to add sound to a photo, while Eraser Shot lets you erase unwanted items in the picture. Dual Camera Shot enables the user to take a picture with both cameras at once, so that you can get pictures of you and your friends at the same time.

The video camera is also upgraded and takes excellent quality video, so overall the camera is one of the biggest reasons to upgrade.

Design

The Samsung Galaxy S4 and S3 are very similar in design, but there are some differences when you compare them side by side. As previously mentioned, the bezel on the Galaxy S4 is a bit smaller. This enables a larger screen size on the S4, despite dimensions that are smaller overall. The Galaxy S4 checks in at 5.38 inches by 2.75 inches by .31 inches. The Galaxy S3 is 5.38 inches by 2.78 inches by .34 inches.

The S4 is also a bit less rounded at the edges, as the radius of the corners is tighter. Since both cameras are very thin at under one-half inch, they fit comfortably into your pocket and won't cause that annoying, uncomfortable phone bulge that some of the larger smart phones cause. They should slide easily in and out of your pocket, as well, due to the smooth materials used.

Processor

The Samsung Galaxy S4 has some of the best hardware on the planet, with a quad-core processor, the 1.6 GHz Cortex-A15. The Galaxy S3 used a quad-core 1.4GHz Cortex-A9, so there is not a huge difference in processing power. There is twice as much memory in the S4, though, with 2GB of RAM to 1GB in the Galaxy S3. That enables more multi-tasking and a smoother interface, with lagging performance a rarity.

This extra power is a nice luxury to have, but most people won't notice it unless they do a lot of gaming on their phone. Some will argue that software is every bit as important as processing power when it comes to the general performance of a smart phone, so the Galaxy's software is worth careful inspection as well.

Software

The Samsung Galaxy S4 starts out with Jelly Bean, or Android 4.2.2. The Galaxy S3 started out with Ice Cream Sandwich, which is version 4.0 of Android. The S3 has available upgrades to 4.1.2, a version of Jelly Bean. Both of the phones use Touchwiz, a custom Samsung user interface, though the version on the S4 is newer.

The Galaxy S4 has a number of added features, including Eye Scroll, Air Gesture and S Translator. The phone is able to track your eyes and scroll based on what part of the screen you're looking at. Air Gesture is able to sense your fingers moving above the screen, so a wave of your fingers can trigger different actions in the phone.

These features sound really cool, and they're fun to play with for a few minutes. However, what's the real advantage of waving your hand in front of the screen instead of touching it?

The eye tracking features also don't work quite well enough to be practical in most uses.

S Translator is an awesome feature if you travel a lot, though. Overall, the software does run pretty seamlessly, so you can count on a phone with reliable top-notch performance.

Battery

The battery life gets a big upgrade in the S4, with a battery that's nearly 25 percent bigger. It goes from 2100 mAh to 2600 mAh, for a 23.8 percent improvement. According to the official specifications, the S4 can last up to 370 hours in stand-by mode and up to 17 hours while talking. The S3 is graded at 790 hours in standby and up to 11 hours and 40 minutes while talking.

Some of that difference is because there is a bigger screen on the S4, but still, the larger battery provides overall gains since most people don't leave their phone in standby all of the time. You will rarely need to recharge your S4 during the course of one day, and even with the GPS turned on and no charger attached, it can run for several hours without draining the battery.

Perhaps the most impressive thing about the bigger battery is that Samsung figured out a way to shoehorn it into a smaller phone.

12

Chapter 2: Getting Started

Turning On and Off

There are three physical buttons on the Samsung Galaxy S4 and two touch screen style buttons in the bezel. The physical button on the right side of the phone is the power button. It's located near the top of the phone. Simply press and hold the button for about two seconds and you'll see the option to "Power off." Once you press "Power off," you'll be warned that your device will shut down. Press "OK," and your phone will shut down.

To turn your phone back on, press and hold the same button for about three seconds. Your phone will vibrate, and then begin the process of booting up.

Installing SIM Card

First, you need to remove the back cover on the phone, which can be confusing at first. Just above the power button, there is a notch in the cover. Press your fingernail into that notch and lift away to pop the first tab open on the cover.

The easiest way to continue is to slide your fingernail down the phone in between the back cover and the body of phone, which will continue to pop open the tabs. Once you have released enough of them, the cover will easily pull away.

You'll now be looking at back of the phone, with a SIM card, microSD card and the battery. The SIM card is on the top right side. To install your SIM card, align the metal contacts on the card with those on the phone. They should be facing down. The SIM card should just slide into place.

Installing Battery

Repeat the same process to remove the back cover on the phone by sliding your fingernail into the notch that enables you to pull the cover off. See the instructions under "Installing SIM Card," if you have trouble. Your battery goes into the big rectangular slot. Simply align the pins and place it in the slot, pressing down until it is secured.

How to Transfer Files from Your Old Phone

The easiest way to transfer the contents of your old phone to your new phone is by simply carrying over your Google account if you are coming from another Droid phone. That will get you the most important content, such as your address book full of contacts and phone numbers and access to all of your apps to re-download them through the Google Play Store.

Alternatively, you can download Smart Switch for your computer and connect your old phone to your computer via its USB cable. You can then backup the files from your old phone to the computer, then disconnect it. Now connect the USB cable for your new Samsung Galaxy S4 and open up Smart Switch. Go to the Tools function and your computer should recognize the phone. Select "Start Transfer," and find your backup file. Select the option to transfer it to your new smart phone and allow the transfer to run. Once it's done, you can disconnect the Galaxy S4 and check to make sure that all of the files transferred.

Transferring Using Samsung Kies

Samsung Kies is a useful method of transferring files to your computer to back them up or transferring them to a future device. First, you need to install Samsung Kies on your computer, then you can connect your phone to the computer with the USB data cable. Select "Connected devices," and click the types of files you would like to transfer. Choose whether to transfer through internal or external memory. Your internal memory is on the phone itself, while the external memory is your microSD card. Once you select an option, you can choose the files that you want to copy over to your computer for safekeeping.

Transferring as a Media Device

Connect your USB data cable to your computer and drag down the top menu from the home screen. You should see an Ongoing notification that says, "Connected as installer." You can either click for more options and then select "media device," or wait for a few moments. After about 30 seconds, it should change to a media device. At this point, you can browse the files on your Samsung Galaxy S4 as if it is an external hard drive and move files back and forth.

Creating a Samsung Account

Early on in the setup process, your phone will ask you if you have a Samsung account. If you have one, you can sign up. If not, you do have the option to either skip it or create a new one.

If you miss that chance, click the Menu on the bezel of your phone, then click "Settings." Select the Accounts tab, and then click "Add account," which should stand out due to the green circle with a plus sign in it. Choose Samsung account at the top of the list, then select "Create new account." You can now fill out the information with your email address, password, date of birth, name and zip code. Once you have filled out the form, push the button at the bottom that says "Sign up." You'll have to agree to all of the terms and conditions and then verify your account through your email address. That will enable you to activate your account and you'll be all set.

Setting up a Voicemail

Press the phone icon from your home screen and then press the voice mail icon. You'll then go through a tutorial to enter a password, record your greeting and record your name. The process may vary by provider, but it should be very self-explanatory.

Chapter 3: Basic Features

Touch Screen

The Samsung Galaxy S4 touch screen is pretty easy to use. It only takes a light touch to press a button and it is particularly sensitive to your touch. The one thing you'll need to be careful of is letting your fingers that are holding the phone brush against the screen, as that could cause some accidental button pushes. There are also two touch buttons in the bezel of the phone that will light up when touched. The left touch button pulls up a fly out menu including settings, while the right touch button is a return button.

Layout

The layout and navigation of the menus on the Samsung Galaxy S4 is pretty simple. You'll start with an unlock screen and after you either punch in your numbers or your pattern, you'll be taken to the home screen. You can customize the look of your home screen with different shortcuts and widgets. At the bottom, you'll have a few buttons that are also customizable and will include a shortcut to your App tray, your phone dialer and your text messages. You can drag your finger across the screen to move to other screens full of shortcuts, and you can add additional screens if you need more room for shortcuts and widgets.

Screen

In order to rotate the screen, you simply need to angle your phone horizontally and it will adjust accordingly after a few seconds. Sometimes you may be in situations in which you do not want your screen to rotate, so there is a convenient toggle button if you drag down the top menu. When it is lit up green, your screen will automatically rotate. When you toggle it off, your screen will stay vertical no matter how you hold your phone.

You can also adjust your brightness from the same menu with a sliding scale. If you drag it all the way to the right, it will maximize the brightness, but this can be a drain on your battery. You can also check the auto button to allow your phone to adjust the brightness automatically to your conditions. This is typically an effective option to use.

Keyboard

Any time that you want to bring your keyboard up, simply touch the field that you want to type into. The keyboard will automatically pop up and you can type accordingly. While you are typing, if you drag the top menu down from the status bar, you'll see an ongoing notification that says, "Select input method." If you touch that button, you'll be able to cycle between your available keyboards. You can also download additional keyboards from the Google Play Store if you wish to add to your selection.

Volume

The easiest way to adjust the volume on your new Samsung Galaxy S4 is to use the physical button on the left side of the phone. That will pull up a sliding bar to adjust the volume, which you can do by holding down one end of the button or repeatedly pressing it. Once the sliding bar is on your screen, you can also use your finger to slide it left or right on the touch screen.

Settings Panel

You can access the settings panel on your phone by pushing the menu button on the bottom left corner of the bezel. Touch the settings button and you'll be into the Settings Panel. You have four tabs across the top: Connections, My Device, Accounts and More.

Under Connections, you can toggle Airplane mode, Wi-Fi and Bluetooth. You can also view your updated Data usage for the month. Under "More networks," you can access settings for your mobile networks, turn your hotspot and tethering off and on and manage virtual private networks.

The Connections menu also allows you to use NFC, S Beam or DLNA to share files with other devices. You can also connect to Kies via Wi-Fi or utilize screen mirroring to send your phone's screen to another device.

Under the My Device tab, you can access settings to lock your screen and adjust your display settings such as brightness and screen timeout. You can also access the settings for your LED indicator, so that it will show different colors depending on what notifications have triggered it. You can play with your sound settings, such as ringtones and notifications, and adjust your home screen mode. Next up are your call settings, which include call restriction and rejection messages, alerts and forwarding.

You can also toggle power saving mode and settings when connecting with accessories such as HDMI cables and docks. You can access the accessibility menu, which provides another way of accessing your screen timeout, lock and auto-rotation settings. In addition, it provides settings to assist users with impaired vision, hearing or dexterity.

Finally, you can play with your motions and gestures settings, smart screen, air view and voice control. These are some of the cool features that your phone has, which may prove useful to you.

Next up is the Accounts menu, which allows you to manage settings for accounts that are linked to your phone such as Facebook, Twitter, Google and others. You can also add new accounts. Some of the options include Amazon, Dropbox, Email, LinkedIn and Samsung.

Under the "More," tab you can set permissions related to your location services and security. You can also manage your battery, storage, applications, date and time and view information about your phone's model, Android version and status.

Chapter 4: Navigating Your Device

Navigating the Menu

The basic navigation of the Samsung Galaxy S4 is pretty intuitive and self-explanatory after you spend a few minutes on the device. There are five main screens that you can see: the lock screen, the home screen, the dialer, the app menu, the settings menu or any app that you currently have open.

In order to leave the lock screen, you can punch in your pass code or secret pattern. That should take you to the home screen, unless your phone locked while you were in an app.

At any point, you can press the center button in the bottom bezel of the phone to return to the home screen.

From the home screen, you can swipe across the screen to move to the left or right screens. You can press a shortcut to be taken to an app, and you can press the menu button and hit settings to pull up the settings menu.

From an app that you have open, you can press the center button to return to the home screen while leaving the app open, or hold it down to see a list of open apps and select one to open. You can hit the return button in the bottom right corner of the bezel or any exit option in the menu to close the app.

The key to remember is that at any time you can hit the center button to return to the home screen, or you can move backward in your navigation with the return button.

Command Keys

There aren't too many buttons on the Samsung Galaxy S4, and the touch screen operation is relatively straightforward. There are three physical buttons and two touch buttons in the bezel, so you basically need to remember the functions of five buttons.

There is one physical button on each side of the phone, near the top. The one on the left adjust the volume of the ringer, or the volume of media playback while you are playing back sound or video. The one on the right turns off the screen if you press and release and turns off the phone if you press it and hold it.

The center button at the bottom of the screen can be pressed and released to return to the home screen or pressed and held to bring up the Task Manager and see all of the open apps.

The two touch buttons in the bezel are on the left and right of that center button. The one on the left will pull up the phone's fly out settings menu from the home screen or an app's fly out settings menu from within an app. The button on the right is a return button, which will move you backward within a structure of menus, serve as a back button inside a web browser and exit an app if you are on the app's main screen.

Palm Motions

You can enable palm motions to gain additional ways to control your device. In order to do so, go to your phone's settings menu (Click the lower left bezel button and select settings) and press the "My device," tab. Scroll down to "Motions and gestures," and press it. Now you can turn palm motion on with the toggle switch in this menu.

There are two things that you can do with palm motions. First, you can mute or pause sounds by covering the screen with your hand while playing media with the screen turned on. Second, you can capture the screen by swiping your hand across it from left to right or right to left.

The muting/pausing effect can be particularly useful if you need to silence your phone in a hurry. You do not need to keep holding your hand to the screen to maintain the pause, either. It will stay paused until you hit play.

Air Gesture

Air gestures enable you to control your phone with the movements of your hand or finger without actually touching the screen thanks to a sensor that is located near the top of the face of the phone.

When your screen is turned off, you can move your hand above the sensor in order to see any notifications, missed calls or new messages. This feature is called "Quick Glance."

"Air Jump," will scroll an email or webpage up or down by moving your hand over the sensor in the corresponding direction. You can also use "Air Browse," to move between webpages, songs, memos and images. To do so, move your hand across the sensor from left to right.

"Air Move," will enable you to move an icon. Tap and hold the icon with one hand and use the other to move across the sensor and move the icon.

Finally, use "Air Call Accept," to answer a call when it comes in. Simply move your hand across the sensor to the left and then the right to answer the call.

Air View

The Air View feature gives you more information about something when you hover your finger over it. It's a lot like using your mouse pointer on the computer to hover over an item until more information pops up.

You can activate Air View by going into the settings menu, selecting "My device," and scrolling down to "Air View." You can touch it to go to the sub menu, where you can activate it with a toggle button and then go through feature by feature to select the ones that you wish to activate. The options include information preview, progress preview, speed dial preview and webpage magnifier.

Smart Pause

This feature senses whether or not your eyes are looking at the screen and automatically pauses video playback if you look away from the screen. You can enable the feature by navigating to the Settings menu, selecting the My Device tab and touching "Smart Screen." From there, you can press the check box next to Smart pause.

Smart Scroll

Smart Scroll will enable you to control the movement of the screen with your eyes while reading an email or browsing a web page. When you look toward the top of the screen, the phone will scroll up. When you look toward the bottom, it will scroll down. You can activate this feature by navigating to the Settings menu, selecting the My Device tab and pressing "Smart Screen." You can then toggle Smart scroll on and control some of the specific options within the sub menu.

Multi-Window

Multi-window enables you to open up multiple apps at once and view them side-by-side, splitting the large screen in half. You can activate it from the notification bar by dragging the notifications menu down and turning on the Multi-window toggle button. If it is not visible, use the block icon and activate it from the menu that pops up.

Once it is turned on, you can enter the Multi-window menu by touching the little rounded arrow that you should see on the left side of your screen. When you do, a menu will pop out that includes all of the active, available apps that are compatible with Multi-window. Touch "Edit," to see the full list and decide what should make it into the menu.

From the list, press down on an icon and drag it into the screen to open it up in Multi-window. Then hit the rounded arrow again and do the same with a second app, selecting which portion of the screen to open it in. Your screen should now be split in half, with each app getting half the screen. You can exit the apps like usual, which will restore the full screen mode. You can also open multiple apps in either half of the screen, which will enable you to close one without leaving multi-window mode.

Chapter 5: Using the Phone

How to Make a Call

Making a call with the Samsung Galaxy S4 is a lot like making a call with any other phone. You simply enter the dialer, which you can access by touching the green icon with a telephone in it and then type in your number on the Keypad screen. When you have the number entered, you can press the green phone icon to start the call.

If you want to call one of your contacts, you can click the contacts tab on the right side of the screen and scroll until you find the person you want to call. When you touch the name, you will pull up the contact screen, at which point you can press either the phone icon or their phone number itself to start dialing.

Smart Dial

Smart Dial is a feature that can save you some time in navigating your contacts list by enabling you to search your contacts from the Keypad screen. You simply start to spell out a name with the letters assigned to each number. In other words, 2 could be A, B or C and 3 could be D, E or F. So you'd spell D-A-D as 3-2-3.

As you begin to spell a contact, they will appear above the keypad and you can press their name as a shortcut to get their number in the dialing field. You can then touch the green phone icon to start the call.

Missed Calls

When you miss a call, you will see a red missed call icon, which is a phone with an arrow. It will show up in the notifications bar at the top of the screen, on your lock screen and in the notifications pull down menu. If you touch the missed call, it will take you to your call log, which will show you the time of the missed call.

You can also touch the icons to place a call back to that number or send a text message, which both appear below the missed call itself on the notifications menu.

From the call log, if you touch a number it will take you to the contact history. There is a green phone icon to call the contact or a yellow text message button to compose a text message.

Receiving Calls

When a call comes in, your screen will light up and you will see the name of the contact that is calling you. If it is not one of your contacts, you will see the phone number. You have four options.

You should see a green icon on the left side of your screen and a red icon on the right. You can touch and drag the green icon toward the red one in order to answer the call, or you can touch and drag the red icon toward the green one to reject the call. That will send it straight to voicemail.

At the bottom of the screen, there is a third option to reject the call with a message, which will send a pre-scripted text message to the person calling you.

Your fourth option is to let the call keep ringing and go to voicemail, and if you press the physical button on the right side of your phone, you can mute the ringtone while you do so.

Conference Call

Any time that you are in a phone call it's easy to turn it into a conference call by touching the "Add Call," button. This will take you back to the Keypad screen so that you can punch in a phone number to add or press the contacts tab to find someone to add to the call. When you make the second call, it will start out as a separate call and the "Add Call," button will be replaced by a "Merge Calls," button. Press that button and you've created your conference call!

Text Messaging

You can send a text message by clicking on the "Messaging," app and then tapping the icon to compose a message, which looks like a pencil writing on a piece of paper. You can either start typing the name of the recipient in the appropriate field or press the contacts icon on the right to pull up your list of contacts so that you can add recipients for the text message.

Next, you can touch the "Enter message," field to begin typing your message with the keyboard. The paper clip icon will enable you to add an attachment to the message, such as a photo from your gallery. You can also take a photo to immediately add to the message. When you're done, press "Send," and your message will be sent to the recipient.

Once you have a conversational thread started, it will show up in the Messaging app when you open it and you can click the thread and begin typing a reply instead of using the icon to compose a brand new message.

Adding Contacts

In order to add a contact, click the Phone icon to bring up the dialer and click on the Contacts tab at the top of the screen. Next to the search field, you should see a silhouette of a person with a plus sign next to it. Touch that icon to add a new contact.

On the new screen, you can type in the individual's name, phone number, email address and other relevant contact info. Once you are finished, touch the "Save," button in the top right corner of the screen.

Email

You can use the Email Automatic Setup Wizard to set up a new email account on your phone. Touch the Email icon on your home screen, or go through the Apps tray and select Email. Next, you can select the type of account that you would like to set up. If you see your email provider, touch that icon and follow the step-by-step instructions to set up your account. If not, select other emails and begin by entering your email address and password.

The wizard will identify most of the settings, but you can specify how often you would like it to check for new messages during peak and off-peak times of the day. You can set it to check on time spans from every five minutes to every four hours, once a day or never.

You can also customize your notification settings from this screen, and when you've made your choices you can hit next. On the following screen, you can name the account and then touch "Done."

Gmail

The easiest way to go is to just sign in to your Google/Gmail account when you configure your phone for the first time, which will get you all set up. If you didn't do that, though, you can go into your Gmail app and tap the Menu button and then go into the Settings for Gmail. There's a button that says Add Account, and when you tap it you will be able to select Existing, to add an account that you already have elsewhere. Simply enter your user name and password on the following screen and then select the Google services that you want to sync between your phone and your account.

Make sure that "Sync Gmail," is one of them, and tap "Next." You're all set!

Chapter 6: Camera

Taking Photos

The first thing that you need to do in order to take a picture with the Galaxy S4 is open up the Camera app, which is a popular shortcut to keep on your home screen. Otherwise, you can access it by tapping the Apps icon in the bottom row of icons and selecting the Camera app.

Once you are inside the Camera app, it is as simple as framing your shot, holding the phone as steady as possible and tapping the middle icon on the bottom of the screen. It's an ovular, grey icon with a picture of a camera in it. Tap it and your phone will take a picture.

Settings

Once you are in the Camera app, there are a number of settings that you can adjust. Hit the menu button in the phone's bezel and select Settings to pull up the menu. From here, you can begin by adjusting the photo size between 13 megapixels and 2.4 megapixels. Remember that as long as you have sufficient space to store your photos, you can always downsize them later but you cannot upsize them without losing resolution.

You can also toggle burst shot and face detection, as well as anti-shake mode. Burst shot will fire off multiple photos in quick succession with one touch of a button, while face detection will attempt to improve the quality of photos with faces in them. Auto night detection can also be toggled on and off and you can adjust the ISO and Metering.

The next tab over allows you to adjust the Video settings, including the size and the stabilization. Finally, there is a settings tab that enables you to turn additional features on or off. You can add in GPS tagging, a timer, a review option and specify what the volume key will do in the camera app. The default is to make it the zoom key. You can also select a method of white balancing, set the exposure value and turn guidelines on or off. You can adjust the default flash setting and voice control too.

Shooting Video

One of the great things about the Galaxy S4 is that it is so easy to switch from taking a photo to shooting video. Simply open up the Camera app and press the video icon on the bottom right corner of the screen. It is a round, grey icon with a video camera silhouette. Once you press that button, the camera will start shooting video and you will have controls to stop or pause the video.

Editing Your Photo

If you have the review setting on, you will be able to look at your photo right after you take it. If not, you will need to go in through the gallery. Either way, once you are looking at your photo you can tap it to bring up a menu. In this menu is an icon that looks like a picture with a pencil on it. If you touch this icon, you will go into edit mode.

Here you have four options. You can rotate the photo, crop it, adjust the color or add an effect. If you tap rotate, you can either use a pre-set adjustment or rotate the photo by placing two of your fingers on the screen and moving them in a circular motion, as if you were rotating it manually.

When you tap the crop icon, you'll be taken to a crop screen that either lets you cut down the photo by a free select tool which you can drag to adjust or by a preset aspect ratio.

The color menu either performs an auto adjustment or lets you adjust for brightness, contrast or saturation. All of the options have icons at the bottom of the screen.

The effect icon takes you to a screen that offers you preset effects such as Vignette, Grey-scale, Sepia, Vintage, Faded color, Turquoise, Tint, Cartoon, Moody, Fisheye, Negative, Nostalgia, Engraving, Sketch art, Downlight, Blue wash, Yellow glow, Sharpen, Blur and Soft glow.

When you make any changes that you want to keep, you can hit the save icon in the top right corner of the screen. Otherwise you can hit the back button or cancel to go back to the photo.

Dual Camera Mode

Once you are in the Camera app, you should see a dual camera icon near the top left corner of the screen. It looks like two interlinking cameras. If you do not see this icon, make sure that your shooting mode is set to "Auto."

Push the "Dual Camera," icon and you will be placed in dual camera mode. You'll see an inset with the front facing camera, which is likely pointed at your face. The default setting puts it in a postage stamp frame, but you can change that along the bottom of the screen.

Now you simply need to frame the two shots and push the shutter button, which is the big oval button, to take the picture.

Drama Shot Mode

Drama Shot mode is a very cool feature that allows you to take up to 100 photos in 4 seconds of a moving object, a few of which will then be merged together into one final photograph. This allows you to see an image moving through the frame in a still photograph.

In order to open up Drama Shot, you can go into the Camera app and tap the Mode icon. You can scroll through the different modes until you see Drama mode. Select this mode and read a quick instructional blurb about how to use it. You can close it, because it's very simple. Frame your shot, with a still background and a moving subject. Now press the shutter button and hold the camera steady while the object moves through the frame. After it is done moving, hit the stop button and the camera will stop taking photos. It will then automatically merge them down into one Drama Shot.

Eraser

Eraser Mode enables you to do the opposite of Drama Shot. You can remove moving objects in the rear of the picture. However, you have to have it turned on ahead of time.

Once again, you'll open the Camera app and tap the Mode icon, then select Eraser mode. Once you're in that mode, tapping the shutter icon will cause the camera to take five pictures. It will automatically remove anything that is moving in the background from your photo.

Chapter 7: Customization

Home Screen

Your Home Screen is relatively easy to use. You can add a shortcut or widget by holding down your finger on the screen and then selecting what you would like to add from the pop up menu that arises. When you make your selection, you'll be taken to a list of the possibilities and you can then choose one to add to the home screen. This works the same way for any additional screens that you add.

If you have trouble setting up and navigating the home screen, you can opt to switch your home screen to Easy Mode. It works well for people who are not as tech-savvy, but still want to get the most out of their phone.

In Easy Mode, you will get three screens to toggle between. The main home screen will have non-removable widgets that give you the date, time and weather. You can then add shortcuts for six apps, which have larger icons to make them easier to see and tap.

The left home screen sets up contacts for quick calling and provides you with phone functions, while the right home screen has room for shortcuts for nine different apps.

Easy Mode will also simplify other parts of the phone, such as the settings menu and the camera interface. You can also switch back and forth between Easy Mode and regular mode without losing any settings.

Simply go to Settings and click on the My Device tab. Go to "Home screen mode," and select the mode you wish to use. Tap Apply and you'll be in the mode of your choice.

Wallpaper

The easiest way to change the wallpaper on your Galaxy S4 is from the home screen. Find a spot on the screen that is devoid of any icons or widgets and hold your finger down monetarily. A window will pop up which includes an option to add a new wallpaper to the home screen. Select that option and you'll go to another menu, which allows you to pick where the wallpaper will come from. Your options include "Live Wallpapers," "Wallpaper Gallery," "Wallpapers," and "Media Gallery."

Make your choice, and you will then be able to scroll through available options and pick your wallpaper. Once you return to the home screen, you should see it in place.

Alternatively, you can add a wallpaper from the Settings menu by going to the "Personalization," section of the "My device," tab. Tap "Display," then tap "Wallpaper," which will be the top choice in the menu. You can tap the screen for which you wish to change the wallpaper. Now you'll once again see the "Select wallpaper from," menu and you can make your choice and proceed according to the above directions.

Widgets

Adding a widget to your home screen is very easy. You just press and hold a blank spot on the screen, then under "Add to Home Screen," select "Apps and widgets." On the following screen, switch to the Widgets tab and you can browse the available widget. Once you make your corresponding choice, any additional settings that you need to customize will pop up before the widget is added to the screen in question.

If you have difficulty making it work, be sure that there is enough room in the grid on that screen to add a widget that is the size of the one that you selected. For example, if you only had one open spot you would not be able to add a 2x1 widget.

If you want to move a widget, press and hold it and then drag it to the appropriate location after you feel a vibration and see the screen that allows you to move icons and widgets. You can follow those steps and drag it to the remove icon to delete the widget from the screen.

Apps

In order to add Apps to your home screen, press and hold a blank spot on the screen and then tap "Apps and widgets," when the "Add to Home Screen," menu pops up. You should be taken into a list of available apps, but if not you can tap the Apps tab at the top of the screen. From there you can browse through the apps until you see one you would like to add, then tap it to add it. Once your apps are on the home screen you can press and hold them until you feel a vibration, then drag them around the screen or from one home screen to another until you have them in the place you want them. You can also press and hold them, then drag them to the "Remove," icon to delete them. This will delete the shortcut, but not the app itself from the phone.

Launch Bar

The Launch Bar is located at the bottom of your screen and functions a lot like the task bar at the bottom of a computer. It is a constant as you browse from one home screen to the next, so it should hold your four most important shortcuts. The fifth slot will be the Apps icon, which takes you to a list of all of your apps. This is not customizable.

The other four slots are, but you'll probably want to make sure that one of them belongs to your Phone icon, which is obviously frequently used. Most people use their text messaging icon as another, and an email or Gmail icon is a popular choice as well. You may opt for a browser shortcut for your final icon, though you could make it anything that you want.

You change these icons much like you move the ones on your home screen. You can press and hold one and then drag it out of the Launch Bar to a home screen or to the "Remove," icon. When you do so, the remaining icons will be evenly distributed rather than there being an empty spot.

You'll then need to add one back in. To do so, go to your list of Apps by tapping the Apps icon. Browse to the app that you wish to add and press and hold its icon. Instead of dragging it into the home screen, drag it toward the launch bar. Depending on where you line it up, the remaining icons on the launch bar will separate to create room. You can move it around until you put it in the spot you like.

Sounds

You can customize your notification sounds for a variety of different events through the Galaxy S4's sound settings. Tap the menu button in the lower left corner of the bezel of the phone and then select "Settings." Select the "My device," tab and then tap "Sound."

Scroll down to "Ringtones and notifications," and you'll be able to customize the noise for those events. If you tap "Ringtones," you'll be taken to a full list of available ringtones. As you scroll through each one, tap those that you're interested in to hear what they sound like. Once you are satisfied with your choice, you can tap the "OK," button to lock in your selection, you can follow the same process under "Notifications."

You can also turn different sounds on and off for less significant sound events.

Lock Screen

Your default lock screen is relatively bland, with the clock, some room for the date and information about any pending alarms that you've set and a majority of the screen devoted to your keypad or other method of unlocking the phone.

You can adjust the settings for your Lock Screen by unlocking your phone, tapping the Menu button and selecting, "Settings." Go to the "My device," tab and tap "Lock screen." Here you can choose your method of locking the screen, add widgets to your lock screen, set a timer for how long it takes to lock your screen and decide whether tapping the power key will automatically lock your phone.

Note that it is only possible to add multiple widgets or even any widgets to your Lock Screen if you have a relatively low security method of locking your phone. The keypad, password and pattern methods of locking your phone do not leave enough room for widgets.

Chapter 8: Browsing

Using the Browser

The built-in browser on the Samsung Galaxy S4 is relatively straightforward. Open it up by browsing your apps until you find one labeled, "Internet"; you'll see an address bar at the top. Tap the address bar to access it and enter the URL of the webpage you wish to view. Type in the URL and hit "Go," on your keyboard and your phone will begin accessing the page you are looking for.

The navigation in the default browser is a little bit clunky when it comes to adding bookmarks and browsing with different tabs. To add a bookmark, tap the icon that has a star in it just to the right of the address bar. You'll be taken to the bookmarks menu, where you'll need to tap the Add button on the top right side of the screen. This will bring up the title and URL of the page you were last viewing, and you can modify the title to your liking. Once you are satisfied, you can tap "Save." Alternatively, you can tap, "Cancel," or use the return button to back out.

In order to surf the net with various websites at once, you'll need to tap the overlapping windows icon in the top right corner of the screen. This will take you into the "Window manager." Much like the bookmarks menu, you'll see an "Add," button in the top right corner of the screen. Tapping this will take you into a new browsing window, where you can surf to another website. You can toggle between them by tapping the two overlapping windows and tapping the site of your choice. It's not quite as convenient as tabbed browsing, but it more or less gets the job done for you until you add some new browser apps or get familiar with Google Chrome.

To share a website, you can tap the menu button on your phone and choose "Share via," from the options. This will give you a menu of different places that you can share the link, including Facebook, Twitter, Email and Gmail. Decide how you'd like to share the website and tap the corresponding icon, which will walk you through the necessary steps to share the page.

Using Google Chrome

Google Chrome can be a lot more fun to use as a web browser, as it does have more features. Still, it does not offer true tabbed browsing, which can only be had on the aftermarket.

You can view web pages the same way through Chrome, where you can tap the address bar and then type in the URL of your choice. Once you've finished typing you can tap "Go."

To open new tabs, you'll see a similar overlapping windows icon in your app, which you can tap to go to the tabbed browsing screen. You can tap "New tab," to browse to a new site in a new window. In order to navigate between the tabs, you can tap on the overlapping windows icon and then make your choice.

One cool feature is the option to sync your browsing between your computer and smart phone. In order to do so, you must be using a Google account while browsing on your computer. Under the settings for the browser on your computer, you can go into "Advanced sync preferences," and check the box next to "Open Tabs." You may also wish to sync your bookmarks. To access those menus, click on the wrench icon in your browser and then hit the "Advanced," button.

When you open Chrome as an app on your Galaxy S4, you can adjust your sync settings or turn the feature on or off by browsing to the default chrome page. This can be accessed by opening a new tab and then tapping the one that says, "Welcome to Google Chrome." At the bottom of this page you'll see a Settings link, which will take you to a screen where you can turn the Sync feature off or on. You can also tell your phone whether or not to receive web pages from your computer when you are browsing.

Chapter 9: Internet

Bluetooth

The Samsung Galaxy S4 offers Bluetooth connectivity for a headset, and the feature can be easily toggled from the notifications bar. Pull the bar down to get the menu and tap the Bluetooth icon to toggle it on or off. If it's lit up in green, it's on, whereas it will appear to be grayed out when it is off. If you do not see the Bluetooth icon you can tap the boxes icon in the top right corner to open up the full list of toggle buttons, where you should find the Bluetooth icon.

Once you tap the Bluetooth icon you'll be able to turn it on or off and scan for available devices. When you find an available device you can tap it and your device will try to connect. You'll then be walked through any necessary options, depending on the other device.

Connecting to Wi-Fi

Connecting to Wi-Fi follows a similar process. When wireless networks are available, you can pull down the notifications menu and tap the notification to view available networks. You can then tap on the network of your choice to connect, and it will prompt you for the password if needed. It's a good idea to check off the "Auto-connect," option, as it will help to keep your data usage down.

Using your phone as a Router

You can also use your Samsung Galaxy S4 as a router by activating the hot spot feature on the phone. First, head into the Settings menu of your phone by tapping the menu button on the bottom left corner of the face of your phone and selecting, "Settings." Tap the "Connections," tab in the top left corner. Scroll down and tap "More networks."

In the menu that pops up, you can toggle "Mobile Hotspot," on and off. Your phone will then guide you through the settings to create a mobile hotspot, which will enable you to connect other devices to the Internet through your phone. Just be aware that this will take up more data from your monthly plan and may cause you to incur added fees, depending on your provider.

USB Tethering

This is an alternative to using your phone as a mobile hotspot. Follow the same directions to get into your Settings menu and tap on the "Connections," tab. Next, tap "More networks," and scroll down farther to Tethering and tap it. If your phone is connected via USB to another device, you can turn on USB tethering. This will share your data connection with the other device. Again, be careful, as you may incur additional fees from your provider.

NFC

The Samsung Galaxy S4 offers Near Field Communication, which is another method of transferring files. This one works between two different phones that both support NFC, so you'll need to be in the area of another phone. Tap your phone icon and open up your dialer, then tap the "Contacts," tab. Scroll to your contact of choice and tap the contact. Hold the phone back to back with the phone of the contact you have chosen. A "Touch to beam," message should pop up on your phone and you can tap the display to begin the file transfer. Instructions on the screen will guide you through the process.

S-Beam

S-Beam is a method of transferring files to another phone. You can either transfer a contact or a picture or video clip. In order to transfer a contact, you can open up your contacts and open up the required contact. Then place your phone back to back to the phone you wish to transfer to and wait for "Touch to beam," to pop up. Tap it and follow the instructions to transfer the contact.

To transfer a picture or video clip, open up the Gallery by tapping the Apps icon and then scrolling to the Gallery icon and tapping it. Tap the picture or video clip that you want to transfer and then hold your phone back to back with the phone that you want to transfer it to. Wait for "Touch to beam," to be displayed and then tap it to start the transfer. Instructions will guide you through the process.

WatchON

WatchON is an app that works as a TV guide and remote control for your home television. It uses the IR blaster on the Galaxy S4 to control your television and it is programmable, so it can work for other manufacturer's televisions as well.

To set up WatchON, tap the Apps icon and scroll to WatchON and tap to open it. You'll be guided through a step-by-step process to find your television provider by country and zip code, and then you can program in your particular television or set top box.

Screen Mirroring

You can turn on screen mirroring by going to the Settings menu and tapping the Connections tab. Scroll down to the bottom of the list and tap "Screen mirroring."

Your phone will automatically scan for available devices that can mirror your screen. If it finds an available device, you can tap it to mirror your screen. If not, you can opt for the more involved method and buy an MHL adapter to run an HDMI cable to your television so that you can mirror your screen that way.

Home Sync

Home Sync is a feature that enables you to store files on a media hub so that you can share them between your Galaxy S4 and other devices in your home. It can be set up to automatically sync the other devices so that files will automatically be saved to your computer or other home device. For more information, look into buying the HomeSync hub, which will include instructions on setting it up.

Chapter 10: Media

Music

You can listen to music on your Galaxy S4 by tapping the Apps icon and scrolling to the Music icon and tapping it. It will automatically list all of the music on your device and you can begin playing a song by tapping it.

Gallery

Your Gallery contains all of the photos and videos that you've taken, or downloaded to your device. Tap the Apps icon and scroll to the Gallery icon and tap it. You can then select a folder to view and browse your various media. Tap a photo or video to bring up some options, including a share button.

YouTube

Tap the Apps icon and scroll to YouTube and tap the icon to open up the app, which should come pre-installed on your phone. You can tap the magnifying glass icon in the top right corner to search for a video or tap the "Browse channels," button to look through various videos that are available to be watched.

Flipboard

Flipboard is a social media aggregation app that should come pre-installed on your device. Tap the Apps icon and scroll to "Flipboard," and tap the icon to open it. The app will then guide you through the process of selecting the content that you want to include in your Flipboard.

Chapter 11: Navigating Google Play

Searching

The Google Play Store is where you can add great apps and other free or paid content to your device. Tap the Apps icon and scroll to "Play Store," then tap the icon to open it. Once you're in Google Play, tap the magnifying glass in the top right corner to open up a search bar where you can search for the content that you are looking for.

Books

Once you're in the Google Play app, you can tap on the "Books," button to browse available books. You can download books directly to your phone, where you can select an app to read them. You can select from a category, such as "Top Selling," or search by name for a specific book that you're looking for.

Movies

From the main screen in the Google Play app you can tap "Movies and TV," to view available shows. You can browse through the available content and tap on a title to view your options. You can typically either rent the video or buy the video. In addition, you can view the trailer and see reviews.

Music

When you tap the Music button, you can browse available albums and songs. The app will make recommendations for you based upon your preferences, and you can sample cuts from each song on an album and choose whether or not to buy an individual song or an entire album. The content that you buy will then be downloaded to your phone and available in the Music app.

Magazines

Tapping the Magazines button takes you to a list of available magazines, and you can decide whether to buy an issue or a subscription. For many magazines, you can get a free 14-day trial.

Games

The Games button takes you to a variety of games, which you can browse as both paid apps and free apps. You can then download a game after buying it in order to play it whenever you want.

Downloading Apps

Downloading apps is an easy process, as you will simply have to tap a button to download and then install the app that you've just purchased to your phone. Just be careful about your data usage, as it can add up quickly when you download apps. Once they are downloaded, an "Install," button should appear.

Chapter 12: Productivity

Dropbox

Dropbox is one of the most useful apps for productivity on any smart phone. If you get an account on your computer, you can use the cloud sharing service to make sure that any important files that you may need on the go are available wherever you are.

Dropbox is available in the sharing options when you tap the share button for any file, so it is easy to add pictures and videos to your Dropbox folder from your phone, easily making them available on your computer.

In addition, you can share folders on Dropbox with other users. This makes it a very useful app and software to have in business settings, as you can collaborate on projects while also having access to the files from a variety of different devices.

S Memo

S Memo is an app that enables you to jot down notes and lists or draw quick sketches that you can save and come back to later. You can open it from the Apps menu by tapping the Apps icon and then scrolling to S Memo and tapping it. You can click the +T icon to open a new text memo or the plus icon with a pencil in it to open a new drawing. You'll then see a grid to write in your content and you can hit save or cancel when you are done. Once you've saved a memo, you can open it from the main screen when you open the S Memo app.

S Planner

Some versions of the Samsung Galaxy S4 will have S Planner listed under "Calendar," but it will be the same app with the same features. This is the general calendar app that you can use to track appointments and such. Inside the app you can tap the plus sign to add a new event, customizing the date, time, duration, location, description and notification settings. When you are done you may tap "save," in order to add the event to your calendar.

S Health

S Health is an app that can help you track your exercise routines, caloric intake and other health related information. It can also work in conjunction with other health-related accessories such as scales and heart monitors. When you open the app, you will be guided through a serious of questions to provide information about yourself to make the most of the app.

S Translator

S Translator is an app that can translate from text to text in a variety of languages and will also use voice recognition to turn speech to text and then translate it. In addition, it can play back audio of the text on the screen. You simply open the app and type in the text or tap the appropriate speak button for the language you are translating from and it will translate accordingly. You can select each language from a pull down menu.

S Voice

S Voice is the Galaxy S4's answer to the iPhone's Siri. It's an app that will listen to your question and then come up with an answer, or listen to a command and then execute it. You can ask almost any question to the app, and if it does not know the answer it will perform a web search and show you the results. To wake up the app if it has stopped listening, say, "Hi Galaxy."

Voice Recorder

This is a relatively straightforward Google app that turns your phone into a voice recorder. You simply tap the record button to begin recording and then watch the audio meter to make sure that it is picking up the sound. When you are done recording, tap the "Stop," button. You will be prompted to type in a name for the file and tap "Save." You can then tap the filename on the main screen of the Voice Recorder app to view the options for the file, such as playback, delete and sharing options.

Google Maps

Google Maps is an app that will look up a location for you, look up points of interest near a location and provide you with directions. It can recognize your location from your phone's built-in GPS and send you into the Navigation app as well.

You should use Maps over Navigation when you are looking for a point of interest, or when you want to force the directions into a specific type of transit that is not available at the moment under Navigation. For example, if you wanted public transit directions even if you were not near a station, you could get them through Google Maps. The directions would instruct you on the location of the nearest station, even if it were miles away.

You can also make more specifications in Google Maps than you can in navigation, such as a specific transit mode and a route that minimizes walking or transfers.

When you have made your selections you can choose to either enter Navigation, which will provide you step-by-step directions or to simply pull up the directions. The second method will enable you to follow the directions by tapping through them, even without active GPS.

Whereas Navigation needs the GPS to be turned on and providing you with a working location, Google Maps will simply calculate directions between two points and you can follow them manually.

It also has a layers feature, which can be accessed by tapping the icon that looks like stacked pieces of paper in the bottom right corner of the screen. You can then turn on a variety of layers that includes traffic reports, terrain, transit lines and more.

Speaking of traffic, Google Maps will also calculate the time to your destination in the current traffic. This can be convenient if you want to monitor it before you leave for an appointment to see how much time you need to leave yourself during rush hour.

Navigation

You can enter the Navigation app directly, which will then prompt you to activate your GPS. You may then either speak a destination, type a destination, enter your home address and navigate to it or pull up a map of your location. Simply tap the corresponding icon to make your selection. You may also choose to navigate to one of your recent destinations, which will be saved.

In the top right corner of the screen, you can toggle the types of directions that are available: Driving, Walking and Bicycling. When you're in a big city with mapped-out public transportation that will be an option as well.

Google Now

Google Now is a predictive search app that is available on the Samsung Galaxy S4. To access Google Now, long-press the home key (the physical button on the bottom of the face of the phone) until the Task Manager opens. Tap "Google," in the bottom of the screen in the middle. This will take you to the setup for Google Now. The app will use your location history and search history to figure out what information may be useful to you. When it shows you something that is not useful, you can swipe it away to teach the app what you are interested in.

Chapter 13: Security

Airplane Mode

Airplane Mode prevents your phone from being able to send or receive any information via wireless transmission. It can be activated most easily by pressing and holding the power button on the right side of your phone. This gives you a few options, including one to go into Airplane mode. Tap that button and you can toggle the mode on or off.

Lock Screen

Your lock screen is what appears when your phone has been idle for a few minutes (depending on your settings) and you try to use it again. There are a number of levels of security, ranging from none to a password. You can change the levels of security by tapping the Menu button and selecting, "Settings." Tap the My Device tab and select the Lock screen option on the menu. The first option is "Screen lock," and when you tap it you can change the level of security.

Unless you have a specific reason for using a lower level of security, you should opt for a medium level of security or higher.

Using a PIN to Protect Your SIM Card

You can add a PIN to your SIM card by accessing the Settings menu and tapping the "More," tab. Select "Security," and tap "Set up SIM card lock." When you tap "Lock SIM card," you will be prompted to enter a PIN. That will be the PIN that secures your SIM card in the future